D1150119

More
Funny Signs

NOW IS THE WINTER

OF OUR

DISCOUNT TENTS...

First published in 2015 by Dalesman Publishing
an imprint of
Country Publications Ltd
The Water Mill, Broughton Hall
Skipton, North Yorkshire BD23 3AG

Copyright © Dalesman 2015

ISBN 978-1-85568-346-4

All rights reserved. This book must not be circulated in any form of
binding or cover other than that in which it is published and without
similar condition of this being imposed on the subsequent purchaser. No
part of this publication may be reproduced, stored on a retrieval system
or transmitted in any form, or by any means, electronic, mechanical,
photocopying, recording or otherwise, without either prior permission in
writing from the publisher or a licence permitting restricted copying. In
the United Kingdom such licences are issued by the Copyright Licensing
Agency, 90 Tottenham Court Road, London, W1P 9HE. The right of
Dalesman Publishing to be identified as author of this work has been
asserted in accordance with Copyright Designs and Patents Acts 1988.

Printed in China by 1010 Printing International Ltd.

Introduction

The modern world is full of signs – signs to tell us when to go left and when to go right, when to cross and where to park. Luckily though, not all are serious and there are plenty to raise a wry smile.

In this book we've collected some of the funniest signs and notices contributed by readers of the *Dalesman* and *Countryman* magazines, from parking for daleks to while-you-wait ear piercing. Many thanks to all those readers who have submitted signs over the years – we hope they raise a chuckle!

WHERE TO EAT

CALVERLEY: There are fewer better joys in life that a good old fashioned Sunday roast dinner. One of the best places to go in the city is the Calverley Arms, home to hand pulled bear and a roaring fireplace. A great day out.

AMENDED COLLISION
REGULATIONS
when in danger, or in doubt,
run in circles,
scream and shout.

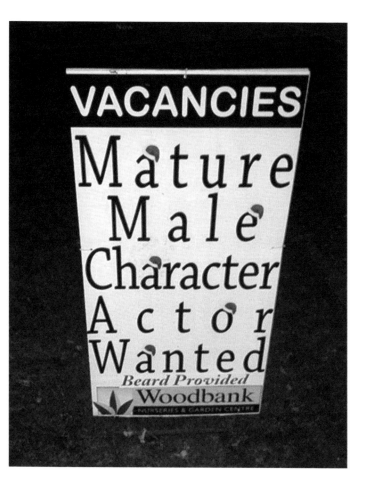

12

Farmhouse Loaf

800g

2 for £2

White bread dusted with flour
Contains flavouring

2 2 4 4 0 8 0 0 0 8 0 0

Contains or May Contain Allergens

Best before
09SEP

1
09

£0.80

100% Satisfaction Guaranteed

Car set on fire

ARSONISTS burned out a car in Thorpe Willoughby. North Yorkshire Fire & Rescue Service were called at 3am on Tuesday to The Fox pub in Fox Lane, where the blue Audi A4 estate had been set on fire. A police spokesman said the pub had been left in the car park by the owner following a night out.

CATHEDRAL BURIAL OF RICHARD III CANCELLED !
(DECLARED FIT FOR WORK BY DWP)

NO ADMITTANCE BETWEEN THE HOURS OF 5PM & 8AM

CLOSED ALL WEEKEND

Gates will be locked between these hours (Horses call at Farm for Key)

PRIVATE

**VAGRANTS CANNOT
TRAMPS MUST NOT
GENTLEMEN SURELY
WILL NOT
TRESPASS ON
THIS PROPERTY**

DO NOT SIT ON
THE BARRIERS.

BELLS NOT WORKING

IF YOU want bus to stop

SHOUT Ding Ding

Bridal way
ONLY

→

**Persons using the
Bridal way please
follow the blue arrows
as indicated
throughout the site**

WEATHER FORECASTING STONE

FORECAST	CONDITION
Stone is Wet	Raining
Stone is Dry	Not Raining
Shadow on Ground	Sunny
White on Top	Snowing
Cant See Stone	Foggy
Swinging Stone	Windy
Stone Gone	Tornado

www.thestationinn.net

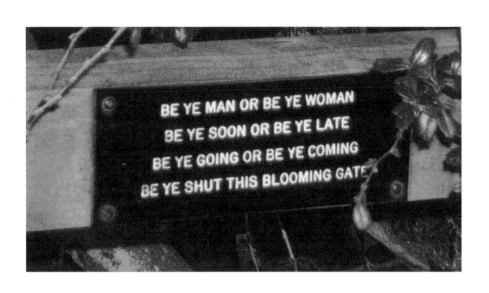

Dales Meat & Pie Company
Traditional produce • Meat • Pies • Sausage • Sandwiches

In the freezer we have:

Chicken Livers
Calves Livers
Glutton Free Sausage

HUSBAND CRÊCHE

IS HE GETTING UNDER YOUR FEET?

Why not leave him here while you shop ?!

FREE CRÊCHE just pay for his drinks !!

74

SHOP HOURS

Open most days about 9 or 10, occasionally as early as 7, but some days as late as 12 or 1.

We close at about 5.30 or 6, but occasionally as late as 7 or 8.

Some days we aren't here at all, and lately I've been here just about all the time, except when I'm somewhere else.

Bruce

In the event of an
EMERGENCY
please jump !

82

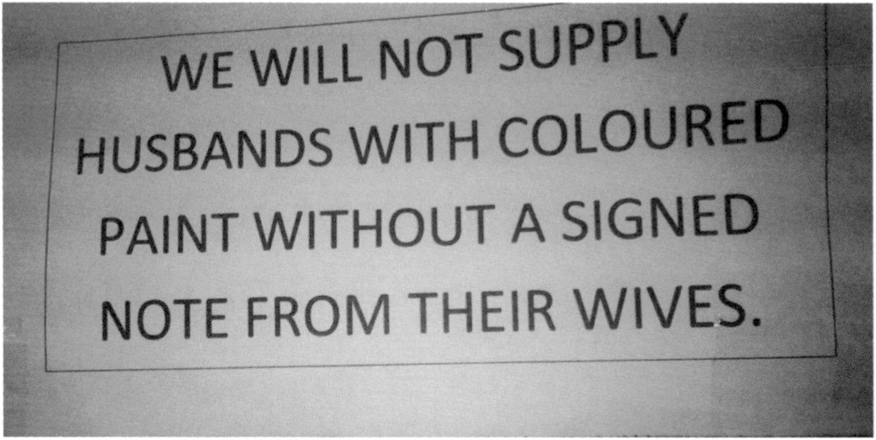

WE WILL NOT SUPPLY
HUSBANDS WITH COLOURED
PAINT WITHOUT A SIGNED
NOTE FROM THEIR WIVES.

Grilled Goats with Salad & crusty bread £

95

Acknowledgements

Thanks to the following *Dalesman* and *Countryman* readers for their photographs:

S Ackroyd
Mrs EM Adams
Ronnie Allan
Elizabeth Appleyard
Derek Ashton
RF Aspin
JA Baggett
Mr D Bagnall
Mrs J Ball
Margaret Barker
Michael Bass
Mrs BG Barraclough
Mrs J Beadle
Mr L Bower
Frank Bowman
Richard Bracknall
Martin Broadribb
John Brownridge
Jim Clarke
John Cleary
Brenda Crossland
Mrs M J Dorling
Thomas Edgar
Lisa Firth
Ernest Fishwick
Mr H Foster

Mr and Mrs BD Furness
Gaye and Dan Gerrard
J Goddard
M Haigh
John Halocha
David Havenhand
Linda Hepworth
Mr J Jefferson
Penny Jerome
Judith Johns
Mr J Ledbetter
Christine Lee
MH Lowndes
Sarah Macmillan
Tony Marr
Mr T Mason
B McLoughlin
Rob Millard
Barbara Mills
Miss T Meehan
Mr D Mitchell
Mrs Rosamund Mitchell
Sarah Mitchell
Mrs J Moore
Harold W Mountain
Keith Parry

Mrs CC Pickering
John Pittock
David Pratt
Thomas M Rayner
Mrs Heather Reynolds
Simon Rhodes
Derek L Richards
Revd. John Richards
Margaret E Robinson
Peter JH Slessor
B Smith
David Sumner
Richard Throup
Frank Tyas
Mrs L Vorlicky
JG Waddington
Bob Walker
WS Walker
W Wells
Ralph Wilkinson
Mr Keith Willmott
J Wilson
Glenda Yates
Mrs Wendy Young